Tina Black

STEVE WATERS

Steve Waters' plays include *Little Platoons*, *The Contingency Plan*, *Capernaum*, as part of *Sixty-Six Books* (Bush, London); *Fast Labour* (Hampstead, in association with West Yorkshire Playhouse); *Out of Your Knowledge* (Menagerie Theatre/ Pleasance, Edinburgh/East Anglian tour); *World Music* (Sheffield Crucible, and subsequent transfer to the Donmar Warehouse); *The Unthinkable* (Sheffield Crucible); *English Journeys*, *After the Gods* (Hampstead); a translation/adaptation of a new play by Philippe Minyana, *Habitats* (Gate, London/ Tron, Glasgow); *Flight Without End* (LAMDA). Writing for television and radio includes *Safe House* (BBC4), *The Air Gap*, *The Moderniser* (BBC Radio 4). Steve ran the Birmingham MPhil in Playwriting for several years and now teaches Creative Writing at the University of East Anglia. He is the author of *The Secret Life of Plays*, also published by Nick Hern Books.

Other Titles in this Series

Steve Waters

IGNORANCE / JAHILIYYAH

NICK HERN BOOKS

London

www.nickhernbooks.co.uk

A Nick Hern Book

Ignorance/Jahiliyyah first published in Great Britain in 2012 as a paperback original by Nick Hern Books Limited, The Glasshouse, 49a Goldhawk Road, London W12 8QP, in association with Hampstead Theatre, London

Ignorance/Jahiliyyah copyright © 2012 Steve Waters

Steve Waters has asserted his moral right to be identified as the author of this work

Cover image: iStockphoto
Cover design: Ned Hoste, 2H

Typeset by Nick Hern Books, London
Printed in Great Britain by Mimeo Ltd, Huntingdon, Cambridgeshire PE29 6XX

A CIP catalogue record for this book is available from the British Library

ISBN   978 1 84842 295 7

Ignorance/Jahiliyyah was first performed at Hampstead Theatre Downstairs, London, on 15 November 2012. The cast was as follows:

NASIR AL-MALIKI / SAYYID QUTB	Jude Akuwudike
LAYLA AHMAD	Laila Alj
WAYNE	Andy Apollo
MYRNA	Scarlett Brookes
PHILIP MITCHELL / PROFESSOR GATES	Dan Rabin

Director	Nathan Curry
Designer	Georgia Lowe
Lighting Designer	Mark Howland
Sound Designer	Edward Lewis

'He had the ability, rare in Egyptians, to keep his secrets.'

Naguib Mahfouz on Sayyid Qutb

'... my job is to write men rather than to write books.'

Hassan al-Banna, founder of the Muslim Brotherhood

For Matthew Carr

Acknowledgements

Thanks to Souraya Ali, Hazem Azmy, Susanna Bennett, Sebastian Born, Chris Campbell, Nathan Curry, Peggy Ford, Fawaz Gerges, Michael Grandage, Heather Keaney, Waleed Marzouk, Ahmed Masoud, Hisham Matar, Kathryn Pickford, Ginger Rinkenberger, Tracey Sedinger at University of North Colorado, Nehaid Selaiha, Jay Trask.

The writing of this play was assisted by a grant from The Peggy Ramsay Foundation and the Arts Council.

S.W.

Characters

LONDON, NOW

PROFESSOR PHILIP MITCHELL, *British, white, forties,*
    (*doubles with Gates*)
LAYLA AHMAD, *Egyptian, twenties*
DR NASIR AL-MALIKI, *Egyptian, forties* (*doubles with Qutb*)

GREELEY, COLORADO, USA, 1949

SAYYID QUTB, *Egyptian, early forties*
PROFESSOR GATES, *American, forties, academic and pastor*
WAYNE, *early twenties*
MYRNA, *American, twenty, student*

Settings

Mitchell's office and the canteen at a university in London.

Various locations in the town of Greeley, Colorado, fall 1949.

There is no set as such; spaces are simply a table and chairs of
an institutional nature which should be common to both times;
everything else is achieved through costume.

Author's Note

This is a work of fiction rooted in fact.

Scene Four contains quotations from the Colorado State
College of Education journal *Fulcrum* (fall 1949); the author
would like to thank the librarians there for allowing him access
to this unpublished document.

*This text went to press before the end of rehearsals and so may
differ slightly from the play as performed.*

ACT ONE

Scene One

October: PHILIP's *office. Sounds of traffic, it's a central-London location. In the room, alone, sits* LAYLA, *in a hijab and long flowing top. She has placed a small Dictaphone on the desk. There is very little in the room, bar the desk, crowded with papers, and a laptop.* PHILIP *enters in a crumpled suit, tie askew. He dumps a coffee and a bag from EAT on the table, eats.* LAYLA, *who has been awaiting his attention, moves into the chair opposite.*

PHILIP. And how did you get in here?

LAYLA. The door was unlocked.

PHILIP. 'The door was unlocked'?

LAYLA. Yes, the door was open, unlocked.

PHILIP. Okay, fine, the door was open, doors are often open, does that mean we go through them? Do you have an appointment?

LAYLA. You wish me to wait outside?

PHILIP. Wait outside for what exactly, given you don't have an appointment and this is technically, I am led to believe, my lunch break.

LAYLA. It says, outside, now is 'office hours' – on your board.

PHILIP. 'Office hours'?

LAYLA. 1 to 1.30 daily. 'Office hours.'

PHILIP. It may well say that but given I have a mere twenty minutes for lunch, during which I was hoping for a quiet moment to eat a bit of – food – and as you don't have an appointment, and as I don't believe I know you, I mean: do I know you?

LAYLA. I was at your lecture.

PHILIP. Right. Which doesn't count as acquaintance – you're not about to tell me I have some sort of pastoral responsibility for you?

LAYLA. You have no responsibility for me.

PHILIP. Right. Good. Well, that's something, then.

LAYLA. I have to talk to you. Urgently.

PHILIP. Urgency. Debatable concept. Personally I'm with Brecht: 'grub first, ethics later'.

He laughs, sits down and goes through his lunch things.

Forgive the mess, I'm squatting in this dire hotel back of Russell Square, no breakfast before eight, fondly thought I'd waft by some bijou Bloomsbury eatery, no, in here at eight to sit on some committee where my dim hope of a pastry and a coffee proved unfounded, hence this squalid *repas*.

LAYLA. I do not understand what you're saying.

PHILIP. Nothing of substance. Mmm. (*Finishes a mouthful of sandwich.*) Okay, okay, you want to talk to me, urgently, and oh, you went to my lecture – did you find it instructive?

LAYLA. I raised my hand. To ask a question. It was not permitted.

PHILIP. Okay, yes, I remember you, sat at the very front, whole empty bench and you – did I see correctly or were you recording me? Don't remember giving permission for that.

LAYLA. My English is imperfect.

PHILIP. Sounds okay to me. Right... ah, and there it is now.

Her Dictaphone is on the desk.

Again. Recording away.

He picks it up, inspects it.

LAYLA. The support team 'granted' me permission? Is it 'granted'?

PHILIP. Yes, 'granted'. For all your interactions? Even in my office?

Might have been polite to ask.

Switches it off, hands it to her.

So, you're post-grad and what – PhD?

LAYLA. Yes. I must change my 'supervisor'? It is 'supervisor'?

PHILIP. Correct. A common plaint. Who've you got? Fred? Rani?

LAYLA. Dr al-Maliki.

PHILIP. Nasir? A fine man and a very fine scholar. Is it some procedural thing?

LAYLA. I may not continue with him.

Pause.

PHILIP. Okay, so you have an objection to his approach, his teaching?

LAYLA. I may not continue with him.

PHILIP. So you said. Perhaps you could elaborate.

Nasir and I have our differences, but –

LAYLA. He criticised you.

PHIILP. Glad to hear it, I'd expect nothing else.

LAYLA. You are an apologiser – for Terror.

PHILIP. 'Apologist'?

LAYLA. 'Mitchell is an apologiser for Terror.'

PHILIP. Yeah, it's very easy to misread Nasir's tone.

LAYLA. His tone was clear: 'Mitchell is an apologiser for Terror.'

PHILIP. 'Apologist'! Sorry, you're saying you actually heard him say this?

LAYLA. He said it this day. I recorded him.

PHILIP. You recorded it. Of course.

She plays the tape. Very faint and in Arabic.

Why's he talking in Arabic?

LAYLA. He insists – I did not wish.

PHILIP. Can't make it out. Right. Talking about my work.

LAYLA. Now, I defend your work.

PHILIP. Very gallant of you.

LAYLA. Now he says you flatter extremes. Now he says you defend the 'indefensible'. Now it is me he criticises, I am a 'contradiction'. Now he says if I wish my beliefs I must stay in the deserts from which he says I come.

She switches the tape off. PHILIP *is quiet.*

PHILIP. Well. That's, to say the least… surprising. But we all, unguardedly… we all say things… well.

LAYLA. Professor Mitchell, I wish you to supervise me.

PHILIP. Right. Well, there we may have a problem given I'm in this joint on a research contract, gun at my head to deliver publications, not obliged nor minded to take on any teaching –

LAYLA. Professor Mitchell, it has cost me a great deal to come to this country to study in this university, none of the things I have done to come here have been done lightly and I do not think this is a mere game of being passed from one doctor to another, I came to this country because of your book, then to be placed with this man is an insult and a confirmation of those who opposed my coming –

PHILIP. Whoa, whoa!

Okay, when you say my book, you mean – you said something about my book?

LAYLA. *Understanding Sayyid Qutb.*

PHILIP. Right. The title is Rethinking *Sayyid Qutb*. And the book is not finished.

LAYLA. I heard you speak of it at the AUC. Your book will restore a great man to life.

PHILIP. I'm flattered by your confidence.

Pause.

So, okay, so, sorry I don't – what's your – your name – ?

LAYLA. Ahmad. Layla Ahmad.

PHILIP. And why is that familiar?

LAYLA. It is a common Egyptian name, common.

PHILIP. You were at the American University – in Cairo?

   Did we overlap?

LAYLA. I do not think so.

   I had to leave – for a while. You resigned – after I –

PHILIP. I didn't resign – well, okay, I resigned because I... got a new job. Promotion, actually.

LAYLA. Congratulations.

PHILIP. What? Oh. Thank you.

   Pause.

   Okay. So what, you've just... graduated?

LAYLA. My degree is from another university.

PHILIP. Right. Which is where?

LAYLA. Is this necessary now?

PHILIP. Useful to know your pedigree.

LAYLA. Jeddah.

PHILIP. Right. Jeddah, Saudi. Wow. You've been round the block. Surprised they let you through customs.

LAYLA. When may we begin? Today? I too wish to write about Sayyid.

PHILIP. Okay. Right. Well, it's a crowded field.

LAYLA. I wish to examine his time in America, in the West –

PHILIP. It's well-worked ground, most of the sources shrouded in mystery and cliché, steer clear of it, focus on more recent Muslim Brotherhood thinkers, or on al-Banna, if you must go back to the source – Qutb's a detour.

LAYLA. No, I will examine his encounter with the West, 1948 to 1949. The beginning.

PHILIP. 'The beginning'? The beginning of what, exactly?

LAYLA. Of *al-Sahwa*. The awakening.

Pause.

PHILIP. Okay. Basic premise here: Qutb was a man, not a saint. Talk of martyrdom, *shuhada*, all of that leads us to al-Qaeda – where we don't want to go, right? Flesh and blood, not a prophet, not a martyr.

LAYLA. Everything I am, I may trace back to him.

PHILIP. If you honestly think that, write a fervid little pamphlet and steer clear of me.

LAYLA. I can write according to the rules of international scholarship.

PHILIP. It's not about your prose – if I were to take this on, and I am not going to, there'd be no sacred cows, no no-go areas.

LAYLA. I will describe how Sayyid saw the America to come, how he saw that all the world would emulate its errors.

PHILIP. You think that? Or did he just see what he was always going to see? Look, there's no documentation, nothing to say that's not been said; if Nasser had let him rot in jail I doubt we'd be talking about him now; unfortunately, he hung him – – ah, you see, I'm offending you, sorry, I don't care for idols and I am very busy, lecturing at two, I wish you the best, but steer clear of Qutb, write something fresher, something a bit more now, leave old farts like me to bury the dead.

PHILIP *is heading out.*

LAYLA. I have access to unpublished... documents.

Pause.

PHILIP. What did you say?

LAYLA. I have documents.

PHILIP. Right. Say a little more.

LAYLA. It is too soon. When I know I can trust you, perhaps.

PHILIP. 'Trust me'? Why, why would you not trust me?

PHILIP*'s phone rings.*

LAYLA. Professor Mitchell, your phone is ringing.

PHILIP. Is it? So it is. Layla.

They stare at each other; the light changes. We hear a choir of women sing.

WOMEN'S VOICES.
    Ah, well, I remember
    Friends of purple and gold
    Friends met in September
    Pledging their faith to hold
    Come friends of September
    Come dear friends of old
    Time shall never sever
    Friends of purple and gold.

Scene Two

1949, Greeley, Colorado, USA.

MYRNA *eating at the college refectory, jotting notes in a notebook.*

SAYYID QUTB *comes in, dressed in a dark suit, with tie, with a tray of food.*

He appears unsure of where to go.

SAYYID. Is this place taken?

MYRNA. Oh. Well. I don't see anyone sitting there.

Sophomores sometimes object to freshmen sitting there.

And technically international students tend to remain... by the atrium. I assume you are an international student.

SAYYID. It seems there are many rules.

MYRNA. Oh, not so much rules as traditions, I guess.

Enjoy your lunch.

SAYYID *nods and turns to a slice of melon on a plate.*

WAYNE *comes in with meal.*

WAYNE. This chicken's drier than a Utah summer. Corn's not much better – Jeez.

Hey, don't I get a Myrna Bailey kiss – shaved special for it?

MYRNA. You smell good! What's the cologne in aid of?

WAYNE. First day of semester and it's an auspicious one. Don't you feel it?

MYRNA. Summer dragged on and on. And I had these awful recurring dreams – y'know, about the Bomb. Scared to go to sleep almost.

WAYNE. Truman said it: 'America was not built on fear… America was built on courage, on unbeatable imagination.' Did you finish your reading prep?

MYRNA. Pretty much. Oh, I ought to return this…

She rather awkwardly hands back a book in a plain cover.

WAYNE. Ah – isn't it a revelation?

MYRNA. Little… advanced for my taste, maybe.

WAYNE. That's not Myrna.

MYRNA. You have to admit it's sort of smutty.

WAYNE. 'Smutty'! Smuttiness denies wholesome human sexuality.

Henry Miller's the exact opposite of smut; the writing is passionate and honest and yes, I grant you, sexual –

MYRNA. Wayne!

She laughs.

We're not actually alone here.

WAYNE. You know what Gates says: any young writer needs to read everything on the block. Oh, did I tell you he graded me straight As for 'Composition' *and* 'Democracy and the Novel' –

MYRNA. That's incredible, Wayne.

WAYNE. Didn't I say today was auspicious – plus he's asked me to edit this new journal – real prestige thing, hard covers, up-to-the-minute American writing, kind of like a college *Partisan Review* –

SAYYID. May I have the condiments?

WAYNE *looks slightly stunned.*

MYRNA. The condiments? Oh, yes, of course: the condiments.

MYRNA *passes them over.*

SAYYID. Thank you.

WAYNE. Actually, sir, I think you've gotten into a misunderstanding. International students are required to sit together in the atrium.

SAYYID. Thank you. For correcting this misunderstanding.

WAYNE. That's absolutely no problem.

Gates'll host the first meeting of the Eng Soc, entirely given over to the journal – oh, and we need a name. I thought *Words for Freedom*… what do you think?

MYRNA. *Words for Freedom.* I don't know. Sits a little odd in the mouth.

WAYNE. Sits prettily enough in your mouth.

MYRNA. Plus it pegs it down, sort of. *Words for Freedom.* Mmm.

WAYNE. I thought it was pretty apposite.

MYRNA. No, it's… good, your ideas are always –

SAYYID. May I ask what you speak of?

Pause.

I myself am a writer.

MYRNA. Gosh. That's a really interesting… isn't that an interesting… coincidence, Wayne?

SAYYID. You spoke of a journal I think. I recently 'founded'…? Founded a journal in my country on topical matters –

WAYNE. Sir – please don't take this the wrong way but this is a private conversation – about a speculative venture.

SAYYID. I see. My apologies. How rude of me.

WAYNE. I don't blame you, sir, I suspect you've been a little misled about how we do things here at Greeley.

MYRNA. He's just a freshman, it's an easy mistake.

WAYNE. If he's a freshman, where's his beanie? Freshmen wear their beanies at all times.

SAYYID. I do not understand... you.

WAYNE. Where's your cap? Your freshman's cap?

MYRNA. Oh, Wayne, aren't you being something of a stickler –

WAYNE. 'A stickler'? Says the gal who passed on Henry Miller. Okay, I quit with this chicken – catch you at Civics, Myrnie?

MYRNA. Sure. Of course.

WAYNE *leans in and kisses her, then goes.*

SAYYID *toys with his melon.* MYRNA *watches.*

I should apologise – for my fiancé.

He's excitable – it's his final year, he's tipped to be head of the student body – Professor Gates thinks he's likely to attend an Ivy League grad school... which'll probably be the end of...

Pause.

That's, that's a nice piece of melon.

SAYYID. It is actually very dry.

MYRNA. Oh. Well, yeah, well, everything's dry this year. Been a fearful drought.

Pause.

SAYYID. Do you like melon?

MYRNA. Melon? Do I like it? Sure, sure I do. Generally, generally I like it with a little salt on it.

SAYYID. Salt? On a melon?

MYRNA. Sure, not a whole lot, just, just a shake.

Just a – my mother says it brings out the taste.

SAYYID. Salt! On a melon!

He eats, laughs quietly. She laughs.

MYRNA. Why are we laughing about this?

SAYYID *picks up a pepper dispenser and shakes it over the melon.*

Hey, that's… that's not… no, that's actually pepper.

SAYYID. Yes. It is pepper.

MYRNA. But you're not going to put pepper – not on that melon? You're just fooling with me, right?

He cuts her a slice. Peppers it.

SAYYID. Please.

MYRNA. Aw, no, this does not feel… right.

SAYYID. Try it. Like so.

MYRNA. Well, okay. Here goes. Mmm. Well – I – oh – makes you – cough – ew – a little. Jeez.

SAYYID *gets up to go.*

SAYYID. This is how we eat melon. In Egypt.

MYRNA *sits alone.*

MYRNA. Oh. I didn't catch your… name.

Scene Three

October, now; PHILIP*'s office;* PHILIP *on his mobile.*

PHILIP. And where are you guys based? / Okay. / Be delighted to do that. / The schedule's pretty tight, yeah, it's due out in the new year, yeah, right now, I'm just tinkering with the proofs – letting go of the baby. / Oh yeah, ebook, hardback but also paperback, we want the widest – right. / Look, I should say I am having similar conversations with the BBC. / World Service, yes, but also, domestic. / Well, good, lunch would be very good. In the diary. / Great.

NASIR *appears with a manuscript;* PHILIP *waves him in.*

Look, I need to. / Okay, look forward to it, look forward to it. Great. Great stuff.

NASIR. You are being wooed?

PHILIP. Entirely platonically of course.

NASIR. How disappointing.

PHILIP. Generally disapprove of academics whoring round TV studios but I make an exception for *Al Jazeera.*

NASIR. And what a baleful influence they have had.

PHILIP. Listen, when the Dean next brings up 'impact', I'll fling this in her face – possible documentary to accompany publication – oh, and in your translation, I hope – now Arabic rights are sorted.

NASIR *(laughs).* You imagine they'll publish this book in Egypt – in my translation?

PHILIP. Listen, this isn't the time to discuss this, I've someone due, let's do this properly over supper.

NASIR. I may not – I have my seminar group then.

PHILIP. Okay, so maybe lunch, tomorrow?

NASIR. Tomorrow; ah, tomorrow I have the interfaith conference.

PHILIP. Of course. Busy guy.

Pause.

NASIR. Besides, I thought you deserved an early response.

PHILIP. Okay. Is it as bad as all of that?

NASIR *gets out a manuscript.*

NASIR. I have annotated it, but my thoughts are less about the book and more about its... about your... wider purposes.

PHILIP. Okay. Might be just a little too late in the day to reflect on 'wider purposes'.

NASIR. Here. Congratulations.

Hands over manuscript.

You know I have found your work naive in the past. Your recent experiences have sharpened your thinking.

PHILIP. Right. Faint praise. Omenous.

NASIR. I suppose I wondered who the audience might be, for this.

After all, in the West, Qutb is barely known, yet here, even as you introduce him you, well, belittle him.

PHILIP. Do I belittle him? I humanise him, demystify him, perhaps –

NASIR. Philip, is this a time for such nuances? For Islamists, his death is still news; they say the Prophet came on a white horse to his cell, that he did not die, no, he became his followers – al-Zawahiri, Khomenei. His memory is fragile, tender, as is the situation. So to have you writing this book, let us be honest, as an outsider, an Englishman, and after your tenure at AUC – I say this only to note your vulnerabilities.

PHILIP. Okay. Thanks. For pointing those out.

Pause.

NASIR. But I have been too frank; my viewpoint is partial, of course.

PHILIP. As I was writing I kept in mind a certain sort of rich Egyptian kid I used to teach; you know, all white cotton, stringy beard like a Bedouin, brandishing Qutb as their mascot; how angry they'd get as I told them for much of his life he was a thoroughly modern guy, no facial hair, no djellaba, wearing a suit, breaking bread with Nasser – I'm just putting the politics back into the man.

NASIR. Even saying so right now would be a spark from a millstone.

PHILIP. Right now is the optimum time.

NASIR. We have seen already Morsi turning on the press, his pet cleric issuing a fatwa against dissent –

PHILIP. I don't take such a gloomy view of the Brotherhood as
you do, they play up the piety but they're just as political as
the other guys. It's the old Sinn Féin thing, stick 'em in
government and the glamour fades fast. Anyway, this is not
an attack on the Brotherhood.

NASIR. Qutb is their thinker.

PHILIP. So let them 'fess up that he came late to them, that
radical Islam was a career move, that he was an opportunist,
bad poet, mediocre scholar, that he turned his weaknesses
into a strength – Jesus, Hitler was a failed painter, right?
Religion's an alibi, always, always.

Okay, I take back the unhelpful… Hitler… analogy.

But, okay, if you fear to do this, fine, I understand, I can get
someone else, someone less good.

NASIR *lays the manuscript down.*

NASIR. 'Fear', Philip?

PHILIP. I didn't –

NASIR. Did I ever tell you I was there the day they shot Sadat,
the Islamists? My father was in the Ministry for Education, I
was seated at his side, fifteen in my school uniform – hair
oiled down, white starched shirt, top button done up tight.
Incredible day. The blinding sun. Sadat in full dress, green
ribbon across his torso. The Soviet tanks rolling along,
troops marching in step with American guns, this, this was a
great nation. Then here they come, the soldiers, his people,
his loyal soldiers, running towards us, and Sadat, he salutes
them! He salutes them, why would he not, he is beloved – he
salutes them as they hurl grenades and empty their rifles into
him, and what did they cry? What did they cry, Philip?

PHILIP. 'I have killed Pharoah.'

NASIR. Oh, I have told you the story.

This book will be a danger to you, Philip.

LAYLA *enters.*

LAYLA. I am sorry, I am early.

PHILIP. No, no, it's fine. We've, we're done. It's fine.

NASIR. Yes. I was just leaving.

He gathers his things.

PHILIP. Nasir, you of course know Miss Ahmad?

NASIR. I believe I am supervising her. When do we next meet?

LAYLA *does not look at him.*

PHILIP. Right. Miss Ahmad, did you not email Professor al-Maliki –

NASIR. I do not make my email generally available.

He starts to write it down.

LAYLA. I made it plain I was not to be Professor Maliki's student.

NASIR. 'Plain'? Not to me. Philip?

PHILIP. Look, there's – suffice to say – suffice to say, Miss Ahmad came to me and – and nothing sinister, I don't think, but she found –

NASIR (*smiles*). You need not say more, Philip. As a matter of fact, Miss Ahmad and I did not see eye to eye – a wonderful phrase; she does not grant me the favour of her gaze even now.

PHILIP. Miss Ahmad. You are in my office, you might be a little more courteous.

LAYLA *looks at* NASIR *coolly.*

NASIR. Yes, let's speak later, Philip.

NASIR *goes.*

PHILIP. It's the graduate's responsibility to make those arrangements.

LAYLA. I said to him I would not return. He lies –

PHILIP. Excuse me, excuse me – that's a colleague of mine. Okay?

LAYLA. Yes.

PHILIP. Show a modicum of respect.

Are you aware of his history?

LAYLA. Oh, we are familiar with figures such as Dr al-Maliki, these 'native informants'.

PHILIP. 'We'? Meaning who?

Pause.

Listen, Nasir and I may have our differences, but they are professionally conducted and that, what happened there, was very embarrassing indeed.

LAYLA *is silent.*

Okay, I have a train in about an hour which maybe leaves us – thirty minutes – so we'd better get –

LAYLA. Where does it take you?

PHILIP. What?

LAYLA. The train?

PHILIP. How is that relevant?

LAYLA. You were in a hotel. Before.

PHILIP. Yes. Was I? Yes. Well, I have a house I rent, now. In a village. In Hertfordshire. I forget precisely where.

LAYLA. Do you miss Heliopolis?

PHILIP. What?

LAYLA. I will write today to Dr Nasir al-Maliki, I will say I am sorry and I shall be very polite, very apologetic.

PHILIP. Good. Do that. Okay. You're more voluble today. Talkative.

LAYLA. I have not spoken to a person since I saw you last.

PHILIP. That's a fortnight ago.

LAYLA. Who would I speak to?

PHILIP. Your fellow students perhaps?

LAYLA. Ah! They speak only of money and clothing and they smoke and drink coffee and are rich and very shallow.

PHILIP. Well... a stark but not entirely inaccurate assessment.

LAYLA. I am not in this country to make friends.

I spoke to a baker, from al-Fayoum, yes, on Seven Sisters Road, and oh, he makes good konafa. Here. Because you eat so badly. Please.

She pulls out a paper bag of konafa, a sticky, honeyish snack.

Please.

PHILIP. That's...

LAYLA. Is this not right? To offer this?

PHILIP *tentatively eats.*

PHILIP. No, not at all, no. Mmm. Well, that's very kind of you.

LAYLA. Please, eat. Here, a napkin.

PHILIP. Mmm. Thank you... mmm, delicious. Okay, we should discuss your first chapter. Which I read.

LAYLA. No, no, you do not like it, it is fine.

PHILIP. Why, why do you say that?

LAYLA. Your face is a clenched fist.

PHILIP. Is it? Oh, I always do that. When I'm concentrating.

Thank you. Very... rich, haven't eaten it in... an age.

Oh. Mmm. Well, look, okay, we can draw some pretty simple conclusions from this – Qutb, in bad odour in Egypt, savaging the British, not as you imply connected to the Brotherhood, simply critiquing the puppet state, in hot water, gets packed off to the States (and by whom? Well, we don't know, probably, I think by friends in government) – ships up in this innocuous bolthole where he's to cool his heels until further instruction – on a handsome monthly stipend by the way – so, so being in Greeley is largely a biographical fluke – and so, yes, the weight you, and those you cite – oh, incidentally, you rely far too much on websites of questionable provenance and your citations are un-referenced – but this weight you place on it is too... too determinist, this thesis that America *inevitably* radicalised him –

LAYLA *is by now taking notes.*

LAYLA. He experienced prejudice.

PHILIP. Oh, right, for sure, Jim Crow, racism, of course, as a person of colour –

LAYLA. He was amongst women – and I think this is it, women –

PHILIP. Nah, don't buy that – in Cairo at that point that wasn't unusual, you've got to remember this was a time when the veil was –

PHILIP *trails off; looks at her. She looks at him.*

– when veiling was on the way out.

LAYLA. Amongst certain women.

PHILIP. Oh, I think most educated, middle-class… remember Qutb was my age when he was there –

LAYLA. Before – he was callow.

PHILIP. 'Callow'? What do you mean by that – he'd written novels, literary studies of the Qur'ān –

LAYLA. Yes. Callow things.

PHILIP. Sorry, you'll need to define 'callow'.

LAYLA. 'The Qur'ān is not a literary text – it is the revealed word of God.' My translation.

PHILIP. Your translation of what? Is that a quote?

She reaches in her bag, pulls out some thin wallet folders with frail-looking letters in them, runs her finger through them.

LAYLA. Here. I think November.

One of his later letters to her. November, I think.

PHILIP. Letters? To who?

LAYLA. His sister.

PHILIP. May I see?

LAYLA. I may not – please.

PHILIP. May not – according to – ?

LAYLA. I am the guardian. Professor.

LAYLA *is meticulously putting the letters back.*

PHILIP. 'The guardian'… how, how many are there of these…?

LAYLA. There are more.

PHILIP. All… unpublished?

She nods.

Then you know they should be made widely available, surely.

LAYLA. They are not suitable. To be published.

They are personal letters – I may only refer to them if I paraphrase.

PHILIP. Sorry, by whom? Who says this?

Pause.

Perhaps, if you need an informed opinion, perhaps I might, at least, take a look at them.

LAYLA *is quiet.*

I see. Okay. Anyway, why would he not like America, anyway? I mean, at that point who didn't, frankly.

LAYLA *takes another letter, reads.*

LAYLA. October: 'The white man, whether European or American, is our first enemy.'

PHILIP. He says that there? May I – ?

LAYLA *shakes her head.*

LAYLA *finds another letter, reads.*

LAYLA. December: 'When the file of history is closed, America will have contributed nothing to the world's heritage of values.'

What he says describes exactly my own experiences.

PHILIP. Oh, your – what, now, here? Really? Amongst the infidels?

LAYLA. No, you, you are confusing… things. Deliberately.

She looks distressed.

PHILIP. You know maybe you need more – support.

LAYLA. I am supported by my family –

PHILIP. Yeah, who are presumably in Cairo.

LAYLA. I am helped with where to reside, he knows the appropriate mosque, the routes to take, what hour to prevent contact with –

PHILIP. Men? I see – so you are in constant contact with who – with your father?

LAYLA. I never knew him.

PHILIP. I'm sorry – to hear that. Just you said 'he'…

Your brother?

LAYLA. Of course, I forward any email correspondence, my work, your comments –

PHILIP. You copy – ? What, you tell him what I say?

LAYLA. I do not need to, do I?

She indicates the Dictaphone.

PHILIP. He – you send him recordings… of our – ? – so you're not actually… this is not about language then?

Okay. I cannot consent to you taping these sessions.

LAYLA *is up, picking up her Dictaphone.*

LAYLA. So. You wish me to destroy this chapter.

PHILIP. Wait, no, no, no – did I suggest that? Okay, I just think, really, that you have a strange impression of what this relationship is.

LAYLA. Guide me, Professor Mitchell.

Pause.

PHILIP. Right. That, that's another thing, call me Philip.

Pause.

Look, all I am saying is there may be a version of this story that is one of hope, about a man's desire to be heard in a new tongue in a new nation. Why not entertain this idea first, why read history backwards, seeing that time through the mayhem of what comes later?

LAYLA. Everything that happens, Professor Mitchell, happens for a reason, even if it is not given to us to know it.

Scene Four

1949. On the porch of PROFESSOR GATES*'s house, a warm fall evening, the Rockies visible in the distance.* WAYNE *is there – hair slicked down, bow tie, glasses, dapper.* MYRNA *is in a fresh print dress and cardigan.*

WAYNE. Where the heck's Ralph?

MYRNA. I think he has football training or something.

WAYNE. Okay, and what about Ken Stockman?

MYRNA. Oh, yes, Kenneth sends his apologies, he's at a try-out for the Little Theatre of the Rockies.

WAYNE. I do not believe this lack of commitment. This is incredibly embarrassing, at Professor Gates's house as well, and I don't even think we're a quorum.

MYRNA. Don't take it personal, Wayne.

GATES *enters with a tray of iced tea.*

GATES. Well, we're in competition with the rodeo, I believe.

Now, do we have a decent title yet? I'm not convinced by *Words for Freedom*.

WAYNE. I guess we're agreed we're calling it *Fulcrum*.

GATES. Is that potent image your own, Wayne?

WAYNE. Actually, credit where it's due, it was Myrna's idea.

MYRNA. I don't exactly know what it means, I just like the sound.

GATES. A fine criterion, I must say. Well, perhaps if there are too few of us we should postpone and maybe review the demand for the journal –

WAYNE. Sir, I honestly do not think this is representative, I –

MYRNA. Kenneth said he'd try to get along later –

SAYYID *approaches,*

Maybe that's him… Hey. Oh.

Hello there.

SAYYID *nods.*

SAYYID. Is this the abode of Professor Gates?

WAYNE. Well. Gosh. Sir, is this your 'abode'?

GATES. Sure it is. I do hope you're here for the meeting?

SAYYID. I apologise. I set off in time. But I became lost.

WAYNE. Sir, I ought to explain, this gentleman overheard Myrna and I –

GATES. Greetings, I'm the chump who received your letter of application, handled your paperwork and read your résumé. Mr Ko-teb, right?

SAYYID. Qut-tub. Deeper, deeper in the throat. Sorry, my English is…

GATES. I tell you, Mr Qut-tub, it's a whole lot better than my Arabic.

They laugh.

Kept yourself pretty scarce. You know, I even think I am intended to provide you with pastoral care – not that you need any shepherding, I'm sure.

SAYYID. Again, I must apologise. For this unmannerliness.

GATES. Oh, absolutely no apology necessary. Find yourself a perch and make sure you have a glass of something, I think we have iced tea here.

SAYYID. Thank you.

He sits and MYRNA *pours him a glass.*

MYRNA. So great. That you came.

SAYYID *nods, unsmiling.*

WAYNE. So, Myrna, we were hoping you might offer us 'The Slender Elm is Yellow'.

MYRNA. Oh, no, Wayne, please, golly, that piece is such an old piece –

WAYNE. It's a published poem, Myrna. We'd be honoured to reprint it.

MYRNA. I just... I feel I have progressed so much and I have this new piece, I wrote it today, it's sort of a departure – I made some copies.

WAYNE. Okay. Of course we'd be interested to hear it.

MYRNA. Yeah, it's awful long, I don't know –

GATES. We're not in any hurry. Matter of fact, I have some contraband spirits I thought I might break out. Bourbon, no less.

WAYNE. Hey, Professor Gates, is that permitted in college regs?

GATES. I figure when you're in a man's house, you drink his liquor. Here. Wayne, help yourself.

WAYNE. Ohh – okay, sir. This is pretty irregular.

GATES. What's good for the pastor, right? Miss Bailey?

MYRNA. Oh.

GATES. Name me one teetotal American writer. And, Mr Qutb –

SAYYID. No. Thank you.

GATES. Firewater of the most amiable –

MYRNA. They don't... drink. Moslem people. I believe.

SAYYID. I drink cognac on occasions.

GATES. Sure. Well, I'm an Episcopalian myself but, heck... no, no coercion. Okay, Miss Myrna Bailey, your latest offering.

MYRNA. So it's entitled, 'On a Porch'. I guess it's free verse. Er. Okay. So.

> 'I had been walking
> Down there by the tracks
> And filling all the little drawers
> In my head with things...'

Skip forward a little, reads kinda long. I get to a house, an impoverished house. I describe aspects of the house.

> 'A rolling shade
> Cut from some rose curtain material
> No pinprick holes
> Among frail, bordering forget-me-nots...'

Uh, and you can see I describe a rug, the cleanliness of the house despite its poverty, well, you can read it –

GATES. Let me read the last stanza:

> 'I watched a fat, squat, slouching woman
> Coming up the sidewalk
> Wobbling in a grease-spotted dress
> Her dirt-streaked, red face showing surprise
> And something like swift anger
> To see me here.
> Her light, bitter voice
> Screamed past me
> Striking on the polished window:
> "Git away from the nigger's house, girl
> You might ketch something."'

Pause.

MYRNA. It's kind of strong read out loud.

WAYNE. It's a whole lot different to 'The Slender Elm is Yellow'. Professor?

GATES. Wayne, you're the editor –

MYRNA. Oh. You don't like it, sir?

GATES. Do you want me to like it?

MYRNA. I don't know.

WAYNE. Is it perhaps a little crude?

MYRNA. It may be. I guess I just described what I saw.

GATES. Do we detect in it what Keats called, 'a palpable intent'?

MYRNA. Oh, you think it's preachy? I'm sorry, I –

WAYNE. I think, Myrna, and I don't like to say this, but you kind of stack the deck. You make the, er, Negro's house, exemplary for its cleanliness.

MYRNA. As I say, I wrote what I saw.

WAYNE. Or maybe what you wanted to see. Anyway, is this poetry or journalism?

MYRNA. Didn't Pound say poetry was 'news that stays news'?

WAYNE. Besides, I'm not sure we want the first edition to appear... I dunno... un-American. Given President Ross's backing, given we intend to distribute to alumni, benefactors.

GATES *laughs*.

But, sir, you must see my point.

GATES. What does it mean to write 'American'?

Sentences tailored to this landscape, perhaps? Sentiments as large as the front range, the rolling cadences of the prairies –

MYRNA. Perhaps the all-inclusive grammar of, say, Whitman –

WAYNE. More likely the burnished Yankee sentences of Frost, not a whit of waste or fat on 'em –

MYRNA. – so what about the liberated prosody of Dr Carlos Williams?

WAYNE. Not overlooking his dictate: 'No ideas but in things'.

GATES *smiles*.

GATES. Impasse. Maybe, Mr Qutb, as an outsider, can help us?

SAYYID. It speaks a truth. This poem.

WAYNE. 'A truth'? Wouldn't that be difficult for you to judge, sir?

SAYYID. I walk around this town. I see every man watering his small square of lawn. Each man alone on his own lawn, watering, watering. Like paradise cut in to a thousand pieces.

GATES. Hard to see the harm in it.

SAYYID. There is harm. But you cannot see it.

WAYNE. I think most visitors generally agree this is a friendly town. Folks going out of their way –

SAYYID. Today I attended a film showing. A boy refused me entry – as a 'Negro'. I explained I was Egyptian; the refusal was withdrawn – I refused the refusal. Yes, I see the truth in this lady's poem. But perhaps my words are un-American.

GATES. Well, as you're not American, you're exempt from that obligation, Mr Qutb. That's an insightful portrait you offer. Maybe you should write it down for us.

SAYYID. Maybe I will. I have something already, a small essay.

WAYNE. We're pretty full up...

SAYYID *rummages in a briefcase.*

SAYYID. Miss Bailey might read it for me so you can see.

WAYNE. Oh, you'd prefer for her to do that?

MYRNA. Wayne, skip it.

She pulls away from him.

SAYYID. I am a child in your tongue. Please, Miss Bailey. Read it.

MYRNA. My pleasure, Mr Qutb. Okay, it's called, 'The World is an Undutiful Boy'. Okay: 'There was an ancient legend in Egypt. When the God of Wisdom and Knowledge created History, he gave him a great writing book and a big pen, and said to him: "Go walking on this earth, and write down everything you see or hear." History went down and did as his God had told him, but sometimes he did not understand some subjects or did not know some things because he was yet young – '

SAYYID. Forward, forward, please, it is very long, very long.

MYRNA. Sorry, I just –

SAYYID. To here, yes, to here, from here, please.

MYRNA. 'Once History was walking and writing in his great book then, surprised he saw a beautiful young woman and a boy she was teaching in a gentle manner. History looked at her and cried in great astonishment, "Who is it?" raising his face to the sky. "She is Egypt," his God answered. "She is Egypt and that little boy is the world who is studying" – '

SAYYID. Yes, yes it is too long. Please, faster.

GATES. There's plenty of time.

WAYNE. Well, I guess I am finding it a little... obscure. I sense it's a fable, an allegory, I guess, but at the moment I simply don't get it.

MYRNA. It's clear enough: Egypt is the oldest nation, the world sits at her knee.

SAYYID. I see, this is a mistake, I will take it –

GATES. The boy – that's us, right? The modern world?

WAYNE. I do not see what in heck I have to do with – Egypt.

SAYYID. You are the boy. Yes, you grow up and you kill your nurse, your teacher, you strike her, you try to kill her –

GATES. Of course, you're speaking analogically –

SAYYID. Egypt was civilised when your people lived in forests. You are the boy.

WAYNE. Sir, now one might find your tone pretty offensive.

SAYYID. We, Egyptians, we came here to United Nations to appeal for rights, and you help England against us and you help the Jews against us again in Palestine, against the justice.

'Oh! What an undutiful world! What an undutiful boy!'

Pause.

MYRNA. That's, that's how it ends.

SAYYID *snatches the text back and stands very suddenly.*

SAYYID. It is of course of no interest, fine, very poorly written work, in my language I am considered a stylist, here, yes –

SAYYID goes.

GATES. Mr Qutb. Mr Qutb, please, come back.

Silence.

Now that's truly unfortunate.

WAYNE. Well, I'm sorry, Professor Gates, but I really don't believe this article will serve *Fulcrum* well.

GATES. Oh, come on, Wayne. First Amendment. Plurality. Myrna, Mr Qutb, your piece on Faulkner, my editorial, a couple of tidbits from composition class, you have your journal. Am I right? And a year from now you'll be staff editor on the *New Yorker* and you'll be bragging to your Ivy League buddies about the roster of Colorado talent you gathered between two covers, now, am I right?

WAYNE. Well. I sure hope so, sir.

GATES. Hard to imagine, isn't it, what it would be like to cross the globe to sit on my porch-step reading poetry.

MYRNA. Oh. I guess. Sir.

GATES. I think it might be good for Mr Qutb and for all of us if he was brought out of his shell a little. What do you say, Myrna?

MYRNA looks at him.

MYRNA. I don't exactly follow, Professor Gates.

GATES. Let's just call it welfare, shall we?

I don't know about you people, but I'm getting a little cold out here. First westerlies off the Rockies. Fall's on the way out.

GATES goes in. They all start to go.

WAYNE. I'll walk you home.

She walks off. He follows.

Scene Five

November, now. A canteen. NASIR enters with his lunch, LAYLA is seated alone eating food she has brought in.

NASIR. Miss Ahmad. A rare sighting.

NASIR eats.

Do not let me spoil your lunch.

You don't consider our catering sufficiently halal?

LAYLA is silent.

I wonder if you can help me – I have spent the morning distracted with idle tasks. Yes, wearisome, the rebutting of lies, but it seems to be my vocation.

NASIR takes out his iPad.

Now, here, my staff profile this morning acquired a most illuminating account of my time spent in the pay of Mossad and the CIA. In it I appear almost exciting. Of course, the old gibe is there: 'native informant'. Libellous, I would think.

LAYLA gets up to go.

It is discourteous to walk away when your professor is speaking.

LAYLA. You do not teach me. I do not accept your authority over me.

NASIR. You are in an institution wherein I am a professor, so that should be respected, I think!

LAYLA stands rigid.

Yes, I was particularly troubled here by the loose use of the term 'apostate' in connection with me. Tell me, do you think 'apostates' merit the severest of penalties?

LAYLA. I am not a religious scholar.

NASIR. Perhaps they merit the full weight of the Islamic law?

LAYLA. I am not in the ulema.

NASIR. But did you speak of these matters in your talk?

LAYLA. I don't know what you refer to.

NASIR. Your talk to the Islamic Society? I make it my business to drop by their prayer room. I even pray there, for I am no less a believer than yourself, despite my alleged 'apostasy'. So I saw this.

He hands LAYLA *a flyer.*

LAYLA. I was invited to give a talk about the future of Egypt.

NASIR. Naturally, I recognised the Brotherhood's slogan: 'Islam is the Solution'.

LAYLA. The slogan is now, 'Democracy is the Solution'. And I spoke in my own person. Or is speaking now a crime?

NASIR. I find the full version more revealing; remind me how it goes again.

Pause.

Surely you haven't forgotten?

Let me remind you: 'Allah is our objective. The Prophet is our leader. The Qur'ān is our law. Jihad is our way. Dying in the way of Allah our highest hope.'

LAYLA. Do you have anything to say to me? Or do you wish to merely insult my beliefs, or rather the beliefs of people who have remained in their country, assisting the sick, the needy, the wretched, serving the interests of their people, not slandering them from afar?

NASIR. What are you really doing here, Miss Ahmad?

LAYLA. I am here to study!

NASIR *laughs.*

Unlike you, I have nothing to hide, nothing to be ashamed of.

NASIR. No, I do not teach you, but I can of course discipline you – if these proselytising activities continue, I will not scruple to do so.

NASIR *goes*. LAYLA *toys with her meal, then stops, weeps*. PHILIP *comes in with his lunch*.

PHILIP. Layla.

LAYLA *gets up and hurries off*. PHILIP *sits down and eats, his back to us*.

MYRNA *enters with a meal and her book*.

MYRNA. Get your *Fulcrum*, new college journal, poetry, prose, short fiction, twenty-five cents.

SAYYID *comes in, sees her, sits a little away with his meal, reading a* New York Times.

Get your *Fulcrum*, new college journal, poetry, prose, short fiction, twenty-five cents.

Do you have your copy, Mr Qutb?

As a contributor, you ought to have a complimentary copy.

Here. I think your piece shines out.

SAYYID. I have published fifteen books and two hundred articles – this is not significant.

He pushes it back.

MYRNA. I guess to you we seem – maybe kind of parochial. Literal.

SAYYID. There is, yes, I fear a literalness, yes.

MYRNA. Oh. So you sense, you sense a spiritual lack?

SAYYID. I would not word it so foolishly.

MYRNA. Oh. No, not so foolishly.

SAYYID *puts his paper down and eats, stops*.

SAYYID. What is this food?

MYRNA. Well. I guess that's beef with grits and gravy, and some corn and potatoes.

SAYYID. It has no savour.

MYRNA. Prime Greeley beef.

SAYYID. Yes, yes, I have seen these beasts in the feedlots, standing in their own excrement. Now they go to slaughter. Men who know them not cut their throats.

He pushes the food away.

MYRNA. Matter of fact, my father works there, the feedlots. Yes.

Oh, I am not saying it is not true.

SAYYID. It was not courteous of me.

Pause.

MYRNA. Why are you here? I mean, you're a very accomplished man, an author. Surely there's nothing we can teach you here?

SAYYID. This is not something I am at liberty to discuss –

MYRNA. I see. So, are you… are you in exile?

What can you hope to learn here?

SAYYID. I study you – are you not the future? Is your present not our future? The wonderful, wonderful West, your technology, sleek cars on interstate highways, towns laid out like diagrams, your culture flickering in the dark!

MYRNA. Gosh – if you're so very angry at us –

SAYYID. You must excuse me, I have had – upsetting – upsetting news.

Pause.

MYRNA. I'm sorry. Do you want to talk about it?

He pushes the paper to her.

SAYYID. They killed a man, the government, the British, our masters. There. A small item! There.

She reads.

MYRNA. Hassan al-Banna. Is that how you pronounce it?

SAYYID. A virtuous man. A man of God, not a man I agreed with, but a founder.

MYRNA. Says it was simply a random shooting.

SAYYID. They shot him, shot dead, as he got into a taxi.

But perhaps, perhaps you are pleased.

MYRNA. Why would I be pleased, I never heard of the –

SAYYID. I mean your country! Your allies the British are pleased, your friends the Jews are pleased, a man of peace shot dead in the street, a man who might throw out imperialists, who did not bow his neck to the West, a most satisfactory outcome.

He gets up to go. She stands too.

MYRNA. I don't know how, somehow we seem to cause offence to you, I think – please, you're upset, please. Sit down. Please.

He does.

I do think for all our faults this country has been a haven – to the stranger. You know: 'give me your tired, your poor, your huddled masses, yearning to breathe...'

Pause.

Mr Qutb, we have this... potluck supper, Sundays, at the Episcopalian church. Just friendship, prayer and good food. I would love you to come; as my guest.

SAYYID. As your guest? How may I do this?

MYRNA. Why not? Why not? I think there you'll see a kinder side to us.

Scene Six

December. It's night in PHILIP*'s office. Raining outside. He's working.* LAYLA *comes in, wet.*

PHILIP. One minute.

She stands dripping. He turns.

You're soaked. Look at you, you're dripping.

Don't you have anything waterproof? I don't have a towel, I don't think. Actually, you know what, I do.

He rummages in a bag, gets one out.

Here. Please.

She takes it, dries herself a little. She hands back the towel.

LAYLA. Thank you.

PHILIP. It's… nothing. Keep, keep the towel.

LAYLA. No. It is yours.

Pause.

You will miss your train.

PHILIP. I'm not going anywhere, working on something…

LAYLA. Your book?

He looks at her.

PHILIP. They're rushing it out in the new year. Weirdly enough, a wonk from the Foreign Office just called – might I be interested in briefing them on engaging with Islamist governments? Actually, probably shouldn't have told you about that, showing off, sorry.

LAYLA. Your secret is safe with me.

The title has changed?

PHILIP. Oh, you saw that. Just a working title before.

LAYLA. *In the Shadow of Sayyid Qutb.*

This title is not well-judged. But it is not for me to say.

PHILIP. No. No, I don't think it is.

He closes his laptop.

Okay, here's the situation, you're missing crucial internal deadlines, and I have to file reports on you and what do I have to say about you, if you simply go missing?

LAYLA. It is not adequate, I apologise again, it is inadequate.

PHILIP. I don't need apologies. And, okay, as for the chapter, okay, let's maybe start with the language –

LAYLA. It is not proofread – my brother normally –

PHILIP. And is he the best person by the way? To proofread?

LAYLA. I'm sorry?

PHILIP. Or maybe he's keeping tabs on you... politically?

LAYLA. What do you mean?

PHILIP. I taught him, didn't I? Didn't I? Samir – Samir Ahmad. Bright guy, brilliant mind, legalistic. Tricky bugger but – talented. Even admired his heckling. How, how's he getting along now, Samir?

LAYLA. My brother is very well. Very well.

PHILIP. Good. Good to hear that.

Pause.

No, I'm not talking about spelling or grammar, I'm talking about your ideas, if they are yours; take '*jahiliyyah*', you bandy around this word '*jahiliyyah*' as if it had general currency.

LAYLA. I will define it better in the preface.

I will define it more closely. I will cite Sayyid and do this.

PHILIP. Yeah, I'd like to know what you mean by it, or rather what it means to you.

LAYLA. Sayyid uses it to describe the general state of ignorance.

PHILIP. Pre-Islamic, yes, pagan ignorance, pre-Mohammedan
values –

LAYLA. Before, yes, and also after, especially now – now in
the world.

PHILIP. Yes, okay, and that's where I lose you – for instance,
where, how, in which part of the world. This is where it gets
vague, dangerously vague. So talk to me about it.

LAYLA. I do so, page thirty. I cite the discussion in *Ma'alim fi
al-Tariq*, in *Fi Zilal al-Qur'ān* –

PHILIP. I'm not after his version, I want yours. Layla? In your
own words? That's what interests me.

LAYLA *looks at him*.

LAYLA. Er... the sickness, in the cities, the constant sexuality,
the corruption, the isolation, the confusions of men and
women and men and men, the rule of man over man, not
God over man, the rule of money and man-made things, the
rule of deceit –

PHILIP. Slow down, you, you've utterly lost me. Are you
talking about capitalism perhaps?

LAYLA. It is far greater than that.

PHILIP. Okay, 'greater' – so what, then – globalisation
perhaps? Or imperialism? Secularism maybe?

LAYLA. Yes. No. All of this and more.

PHILIP. All that and more! That's a very big word indeed.

LAYLA. Now I think you are taunting me.

PHILIP. But really, where does it stop? I am genuinely curious
as to where you think it starts and ends? The Industrial
Revolution? The end of the caliphate? Camp David, the Oslo
Accords? Or where on this earth, now, is it to be found – in
Dubai, Jeddah, New York, London, Cairo – where exactly
does it end, this *jahiliyyah*? Everywhere? Nowhere? Or is it
inside us? And if so, can we renounce it? Or maybe it's a
terminal condition?

LAYLA. I have to use this word, it is not translatable, it is full
of meaning –

PHILIP. – and other words like 'jihad', sloppily applied –

LAYLA. These are Sayyid's –

PHILIP. Refer to him by his surname! Always, without
exception, by his *full name* – yes, these words, they're
replacing your thoughts, your own thoughts and what we do,
we place words at a distance from ourselves, put them in
question, this is scholarship, we test words against
experience and they are invariably found wanting –

LAYLA. Sayyid had experiences in Amrika, in Nasser's gaols,
he had every experience and from these experiences he
found words and he defined them and his definitions are still
warranted by God.

PHILIP. 'God'?

There's a word I never expected to hear in this room.

Pause.

LAYLA. If you wish me to cease what I am doing, if you
consider me a bad student, if I have done wrong to you as a
student, then discipline me. I am trying... I am trying very
hard, I am reading things, everything I read, I read and read,
I read so many books the words are beneath the lids of my
eyes at night like stars seen through a tent, I awake with the
words in my mouth and they are not simply words they are
calls... to action.

Pause.

PHILIP. Right. So, so: what, what sort of action?

LAYLA. To make the world whole again.

PHILIP. Okay. And who... who is stopping it being whole?

LAYLA. The *jahil*. Of course. Of course.

Pause.

PHILIP. I don't think this is working out.

I don't even know if this is good for you, if I am any good
for you. Actually.

Pause.

We could organise some sort of refund of your fees, maybe
you could go back, I dunno, to Jeddah, maybe there you
might find the sort of receptive audience you need... because.
Because I have to be honest, I don't think this is scholarship, I
think this is propaganda. And I'm sorry to say so.

Because I think you're better than that.

Silence. LAYLA *reaches into her carrier bag and brings out
a box file.*

LAYLA. Some are hard to read. I have been instructed in to
how to read his script. If you quote them, it will be evident I
have assisted.

LAYLA *toys with the box file. She takes out some letters.*

These concern his studies.

She puts some letters on his desk.

These, his outgoings. These, his lodgings.

And these are lists of his reading, these are where he requests
things from home.

She puts more letters on his desk.

Enough. That is all.

No one, no one must know my role in this!

LAYLA *stands up, eyes full of tears.* PHILIP *is
flabbergasted.*

Do you celebrate the Christian festival of Christmas?

PHILIP. What?

LAYLA. Merry Christmas, Professor Mitchell.

She leaves the box file on the desk, goes.

Blackout.

Interval.

ACT TWO

Scene One

Night-time, late fall. Outside the First Episcopalian Church Hall, Greeley. Through a door, soft lights, the glow of a party, the odd shadow of a dancer. Swing music plays.

SAYYID *stands;* GATES *comes out to him, watches.*

GATES. As if the Bible itself came to Greeley.

SAYYID. Ah!

GATES. My apologies. You're awaiting someone.

SAYYID. Not at all. Who would I be waiting for?

Pause.

GATES. Over there's the house of our founder Nathan Meeker – right across the street. Now, did you know he was born in Cairo?

SAYYID. Impossible.

GATES. Oh no, Cairo, all right. Admittedly Cairo, Illinois. (*Laughs.*)

I am sorry, Mr Qutb, I've a penchant for a lousy gag.

All great civilisations rise on the banks of rivers – so sayeth Meeker; came here to found a new Thebes in America, a shining city.

SAYYID. Most interesting – but I must return to my work, thank you.

GATES. I'd like to hear a little more about that – your work. Was it mission that brought you to Greeley?

SAYYID. I did not come for religious instruction.

GATES. Oh, it's certainly not obligatory. We're pretty ecumenical here.

Are we not finally all 'People of the Book', Mr Qutb?

MYRNA *enters*.

MYRNA. Sorry. I got held up. I am sorry, Mr Qutb.

GATES. Ah. Your date.

MYRNA. No, no, I…

GATES. Oh, just kidding. Yes, we're just getting going here. Drinks and eats and, oh, I hear the music's playing.

Service is later, I'd be keen to see how we compare.

SAYYID. 'Compare'?

GATES. With Friday prayers? I mean, in our manner of proceeding?

SAYYID. There is no meaningful comparison.

GATES. We do tend to keep our shoes on.

MYRNA. That's probably no bad thing.

GATES. Oh, and I believe Miss Bailey would only be welcome were she to be covered up in something a little less revealing. Which, speaking for myself, would seem a great shame.

MYRNA. There must be – er – congruences, er connections.

SAYYID. Matters of historical accident – and now I really must say goodnight –

GATES (*steering* SAYYID *off*). Oh no, you don't slip away without the full tour, I'm sure you'll concur our church is quite a feat of architecture, not least when you consider the people of this town were dirt poor – the nave is impressive, as are the original windows. I believe in the early mosques, the eastern orientation was shared with the Christian basilica…

They're gone. WAYNE *enters. He's been drinking.*

WAYNE. Hey – why d'you walk off like that?

MYRNA. Sorry. Conscious of the time, is all.

WAYNE. Wasn't aware there was any hurry. God, you look – fragrant tonight.

Smell fragrant too. I buy you that scent?

MYRNA. No, I... Hey, not so close.

WAYNE. Oh why not? Oh God, Myrnie, you sure do it to me.

MYRNA. Wayne.

WAYNE. Don't you think we're ready – to move to the next level?

MYRNA. What can that mean? Hey, quit that.

WAYNE *dives in to kiss her, she pulls away.*

Whew! You been hitting the liquor?

WAYNE. Just oiling the mechanism. What, don't you like the smell?

MYRNA. This is not the moment.

WAYNE. Why not? No one's looking and I'm real hungry.

He kisses her and presses himself against her; she pushes him off.

MYRNA. Hey! Cool it off. Now, look at my, look at my lipstick.

WAYNE. Hey now, Myrnie, did you feel me? I mean... really.

MYRNA. I don't know nor do I wish to know what you're talking about.

She re-makes herself up.

WAYNE. I think you did. I think any girl would.

MYRNA. I'm not any girl.

WAYNE. That's true. But I didn't have you down as a prick-tease, Myrna.

MYRNA *slaps his face.*

Hey – what's that about? Hey, that actually hurt.

MYRNA. I'm not merchandise from some hardware store.

GATES *re-enters with* SAYYID. *They sense the scene.*

GATES. I'm no secularist myself but I do find it a challenge to imagine how a faith founded in the first millennium might serve as a blueprint for a modern society – oh, will you excuse me, Mr Qutb – Wayne, have you been drinking?

WAYNE. Ginger beer is all.

GATES. We don't expect seniors to set a bad example.

WAYNE. Guess you're a little more stringent tonight.

GATES. This is the Lord's house, Wayne. Forget that, and our distinguished guest might justly doubt the profundity of our convictions.

WAYNE. Sure hate for that to happen.

WAYNE *leaves. Music starts up, 'Baby, It's Cold Outside'.*

GATES. You don't permit music within the context of worship?

SAYYID. It is a distraction.

GATES. But an agreeable one nonetheless. Songs from the shows. Ah, yes. *Neptune's Daughter.* Esther Williams. Priceless.

They listen.

Ingenious, the way the two voices intertwine. He seduces, she does not quite resist. Now, surely you two will step inside and take the floor.

MYRNA. Sir, I believe dancing is against Mr Qutb's religion.

GATES. There's not a religion in the world that sets its face against dancing. What about the dervishes? All that whirling?

SAYYID. The dervish dances to escape his body, not excite it.

GATES. Well, I need to set an example. Do follow on.

GATES *goes in; shadows of dancers fall on* MYRNA *and* SAYYID, *who stand in silence; the song plays on, horribly pertinent.*

MYRNA. I don't think you said where you came from. I mean, yes, in Egypt. I just mean where – Cairo? Because that's the capital, right?

SAYYID. I live, now, yes, in Cairo.

MYRNA. Figures. I was never strong at geography. Never been out of Colorado.

Pause.

SAYYID. I was born in a village.

A village far up the Nile.

MYRNA. Right. And I guess it's unimaginably hot there?

SAYYID. It is hot. Not unimaginably so.

MYRNA. But with all that, what, sand, desert – but how do, how do the people live?

SAYYID. In fact it is green. In fact the earth is black from the floods. In fact it is... civilised.

MYRNA. Oh, I didn't mean to suggest –

SAYYID. Civilised, even as we live like beasts.

We pray to Allah, and we fear spirits.

We seek the blessing of both saints and sheikhs.

We learn the Qur'ān in the village school, then in the government school we learn arithmetic and military exercises and how to hate ourselves quite thoroughly. This is... my land. River and desert. Suffering and joy. Ancient and modern. All, all is confusion.

They look at each other.

As it is here, in belief, in life.

MYRNA. Oh, belief, belief here means so many different things. Look down this street – all the churches: the Pentecostal, there, the Lutheran, on the corner that's the First Christian, downtown the Congregationalist, Baptist, Methodist –

SAYYID. How confusing for you. And for God.

MYRNA. For God? What a strange thing to say. Surely Islam has divisions…

SAYYID. No! Islam is tawhid. One. The oneness of God. Of God, man, the world. I don't know why I came tonight and now I must leave.

MYRNA. Oh, please don't, Sayyid.

MYRNA *holds him back;* SAYYID *looks at her, astonished; she lets go. The song plays on;* GATES *comes out with glasses of hot punch.*

GATES. Okay, here we go. One for you and – non-alcoholic.

MYRNA. We were, we were just talking about all the churches, the denominations, Pastor.

GATES. Oh yes, the glory of our church lies in its diversity; here in Greeley especially, city of the saints, well, we all love God after our particular fashion… some of us like to sing, some don't, some kneel at an altar, others deplore altars, some of us think God is one thing, others believe in his Trinity –

SAYYID. There is only one truth.

GATES. Maybe so, but it can be known in many different ways. Folks in this country come from all over the world and they bring what they love with them … we have to practise tolerance.

SAYYID. Or ignorance.

WAYNE *returns, smoking a cigar, taking a nip from a hip flask.*

GATES. Wayne. You're really quite the bohemian tonight.

WAYNE. Drowning my sorrows.

GATES. I don't think you can have too many of them.

WAYNE. Didn't think so. Can I offer you a smoke, sir?

GATES. I'm not sure that would be appropriate.

WAYNE. Why the heck not? We all look up to you, admire your liberality. Myrna does. She really takes that to heart. Things you ask her to do, extra-curricular activities like reaching out, say – to the minority student.

MYRNA. Wayne!

GATES. You seem a little short on discretion tonight.

WAYNE. We all get nights like that. Except Mr Qutb. He likes to stay all inscrutable.

The music stops.

GATES. So, the dancing is done, the supper commences – and I believe we have cupcakes, cookies, hot rolls and – club sandwiches. Come on in and feast. 'Love bade me welcome.'

He goes in.

WAYNE. Cigar, Mr Koteb? Made in Cuba, I believe, rolled on the dark thighs of Cuban girls. Imagine that. I like to.

SAYYID *shakes his head;* WAYNE *blows out smoke.*

Your loss.

WAYNE *puts his arm around* MYRNA.

Oh, did you know, Mr Koteb, Myrna and I were dating?

MYRNA (*shakes him off*). Wayne, let's talk about this later.

WAYNE. Oh, sorry, speaking out of turn, sorry – my mistake.

So how d'you like your piece?

Did we do you proud? Whole campus's talking about it. People come up to me, say, 'Now, Wayne, what in heck is this about?' I say, 'You know what – it's all about me.' Am I right? That I personally kicked mud in the eye of Egypt. Spat in the eye of an ancient land.

SAYYID. Please, you are not... sober.

WAYNE. Oh, and not to be unduly critical, but don't you think it's borderline anti-Semitic? I mean, I happen to think, as does our President, President Truman, I happen to think the Jewish people surely have a right to a land after the suffering they endured and where better than the Holy Land –

SAYYID. Truly. You know nothing of what you speak.

WAYNE. Okay. Nothing. Right! You sure don't hold back, no fear nor favour, right on the nose. Pow!

MYRNA. I really think we should go in. The eats are good.

WAYNE. Sounds good; you really ought to taste Myrna's muffins. I can vouch for the flavour.

SAYYID. I am not hungry.

WAYNE. Hey, he's not hungry, Myrna.

Incidentally, Mr Koteb, I never did discover why you're here? I guess you don't have colleges like this in Egypt, universities?

SAYYID. My friend, *Al-Azhar* is the oldest university in the world.

WAYNE. Oh, right, silly me, older again, always the way, Ancient Egypt. Okay, and you teach hieroglyphs and pyramids and, like, mummification?

MYRNA. Wayne thinks he's being humorous –

WAYNE. Hey, just messing around, come on, Mr Koteb can take a joke, can't he? Yes, so maybe I could go to one of your colleges in Egypt, right, and get myself a little Egyptian action? What do you say?

SAYYID. You are drunk and foolish and ignorant.

WAYNE. Oh, excuse me? Excuse me, sir?

MYRNA. You absolutely are, Wayne, and you're making an ass out of yourself –

WAYNE. Just, you come to my college, now you're hitting on my girl, I mean, you are still my girl, right, Myrna?

MYRNA. Stop this, stop this right now – you know I'm not doing this for that –

Pause.

SAYYID. Doing what? What – what do you do?

MYRNA. Nothing – I didn't mean –

WAYNE. No, come on, you know what's going on, I just figure it's only fair and just if I can go to, what is it, Cairo, right, Cairo, Egypt, and hit on one of your Arab girls, you do have a girlfriend back home, Mr Qutb –

SAYYID. *Jahiliyyah, jahiliyyah, jahiliyyah.*

SAYYID glares at WAYNE with a sort of radiant defiance, walks into the night.

GATES re-enters.

GATES. What's happened?

MYRNA. What's the problem, Wayne, can't you stand a little competition?

She walks off.

WAYNE. Hey – then don't mess me around – don't – Myrna!

GATES watches.

I don't know… I honestly don't know what –

GATES. You ought to be an ambassador for your country.

Not some jumped-up kid in a grown man's suit hitting on the little guy.

GATES goes in. WAYNE stands.

WAYNE. Sir. Pastor Gates. Sir. Sir.

Now a choir sings a hymn, slightly shakily.

May I be permitted to apologise, sir?

Scene Two

January, PHILIP*'s office. It is a mess. Papers on the floor.*
PHILIP *is working.* NASIR *comes in.*

NASIR. There were rumours you had disappeared.

PHILIP. Nasir. I'm... Look, I'm pretty busy.

NASIR. I see that. The final stages?

PHILIP. I wish, I fucking wish. Is it something quick?

NASIR. No, not really.

PHILIP. Bang me over an email.

NASIR. I have sent you numerous emails. I have come to your
    office on numerous occasions.

PHILIP. Okay, okay. I'm sorry.

    I'm... I'm. I'm fine, I'm just – very busy.

NASIR. You are in the closing stages, always the worst.

PHILIP. If I don't sign it off tonight I'll fuck up my research
    submission, reason they hired me, lose the serialisation, the
    documentaries, the public-lecture series, blow out the
    foreign-policy conference in Georgetown, the Arab history
    conference in – wherever that was – unplugged email,
    offline, but still, still – no headway – this stuff, all of this
    stuff... screwing me up.

    He pulls from his briefcase a huge wad of letters.

    Like this, okay, October, yes, he arrives: 'The women,
    young. Clothes tight. Breasts like weapons. Everywhere you
    look.' Confirming the anti-Western line from the get-go?
    Given I argue against that – okay, maybe I can use it. But
    then, hang on, this here, later that month: 'Must belief be
    about refusal? Here worship and pleasure are one.
    Sickening.' What's that, are we talking 'spiritual crisis' now,

that's a three-sixty in the whole… thesis – and what the fuck's this: 'Beauty beauty beauty. In the desert. Nothing but myself.' I mean, what does even that mean?

NASIR. Philip, where did you obtain these from?

PHILIP. Plus there have to be more, have to be, although this is plenty enough to fuck the book up, but not enough to say anything – clear – and you can't discount it, not now, but I don't actually know how to even read them; I mean, do you think she's playing me?

NASIR. You're not still seeing her?

Are you privy to her whereabouts?

PHILIP. Not top of my priorities.

NASIR. As a colleague, a friend, I'd hoped you would at the least support and register my concerns about Miss Ahmad with the Dean.

PHILIP. If you wish to register concerns I won't stop you –

NASIR. Might it not seem a little odd to do so unilaterally?

PHILIP. I give the student the benefit of the doubt before I tell tales out of school –

NASIR. So when she blows herself up and you are on CNN, you'll understand why I will have little compunction in rehearsing this conversation –

PHILIP. Gosh, Nasir, I'd no idea you had such a lurid imagination –

NASIR. Philip, my friend, you know the classic indices of radicalisation. Leave aside the obligatory headscarf, what of the self-isolation of the student, or perhaps the dependence on certain mosques or maybe a certain repetitive piety of speech, but then I would think the most telling indicator might be an extended crush on Sayyid Qutb –

PHILIP. No evidence of any tendency to violence!

NASIR. None, other than her specialising in the theory of violence.

PHILIP. Oh, come on, Qutb never hurt a soul –

NASIR. Merely formed an armed militia –

PHILIP. In prison, subjected to hideous torture –

NASIR. I judge a man by his followers.

PHILIP. Is anything served by anathemas? Maybe, maybe we should entertain the possibility of dialogue before foreclosing on it, huh?

NASIR. In my experience, dialogue requires two willing partners, not one with a gun to the other's temple.

PHILIP. She wishes to study! Which is not yet a crime. And I think my task is very simple, in fact. My task is to teach her, actually. To teach doubt, to teach the art of questioning, that, finally is my task.

NASIR. Very noble, Philip. But have you considered what happens if she is not susceptible to your pedagogy?

Pause.

You won't have seen the campaign on Facebook.

He finds something on his iPad.

PHILIP. Please, I don't have time for this.

NASIR. Here, a petition for the pair of us to be disciplined.

PHILIP. I'm meant to submit tomorrow, signed off, locked down –

NASIR. Let me précis it for you. I am accused of peddling Western ideology, apostasy, Islamophobia, the usual list, you are accused of abusing your position –

PHILIP. Fine, okay, point taken, thank you, goodbye.

NASIR. – that during your tenure in Cairo you informed on your students, that your track record with this may well explain your sudden arrival in London with the outbreak of the uprising.

Pause.

PHILIP. What?

If that's a joke it's not a very funny joke.

NASIR. I assure you it is no joke.

PHILIP *takes the iPad, reads.*

PHILIP. That's – that's – libel. This post was in the pipeline for a year –

NASIR. You don't have to argue your case to me.

PHILIP. I was out on Tahrir Square, I blogged about it, this is…

NASIR. There are case studies of the fate of your students. One, her brother. I'm sure the allegations of torture are unfounded –

PHILIP. Allegations of – ?

NASIR. – they manipulate what are often the mildest of reprimands into atrocities, all part of the emotional blackmail.

Let us frame a robust online response, then go to the Dean and suggest she contact the authorities. Layla Ahmad should at the very least be suspended from this institution; I would argue for deportation. This is now a matter for the police.

Pause.

Philip?

The Dean is still here. We could catch her now.

Philip?

Pause.

PHILIP. All this fear.

We've all been very afraid, for years. Afraid of them, their plans, their passions. But all this fear, what has it solved?

They look at each other.

NASIR. You do not intend to meet with her again?

PHILIP. I know too much to stop, too little to go on.

PHILIP *goes back to work, typing away.* NASIR *stands.*

NASIR. I dislike rehearsing what happened to me, to my… wife.
I reflect our misfortunes occurred under a 'secular' regime,
yes, the hated 'strongman' Mubarak, friend of the West, of
America. But even then, such was their reach, their links
amongst the lawyers, the clerics, then the fatwa against me –
and what was my crime: I dared to criticise the rise of
Islamism. I dared to point out that the veil was nowhere made
obligatory in the Qur'ān. I dared to suggest Islam was a belief
not a blueprint for government. I dared to suggest that it
might be inappropriate to install mosques in hospitals, that
shariah law was an anachronism. Oh yes, Philip, this was
during the great time of repression of the Brotherhood and yet
still they had me declared apostate, that my dear wife was
obliged to divorce me under Islamic law – calling for my
execution during Friday prayers! The indifferent and dilatory
police 'protection', every bearded young man a potential
assassin. And all this was when they were persecuted, when
they were illegal, when they were the so-called victims! Then
do you wonder I fear now more than then?

Pause.

No need to rehearse this to you, you know how the story
ends, no necessity to relate our breach, my exile, her – well,
she felt I sacrificed her on the altar of my work, maybe so,
maybe so. The friends fall away, life is nothing but vigilance,
this is not life, not life.

Pause.

Good, good, publish your book. But I do not think you
understand the terrible beauty of devotion, this infatuation
with God. You think of Qutb as an intellectual like yourself,
you don't begin to plumb the passion of the man, this is
perhaps the problem with you liberals – you can only
imagine the minds of other liberals. But, how, how does one
negotiate with people who think with their blood?

Scene Three

Now it's GATES*'s office in Greeley. He is at his desk.* MYRNA *stands.*

MYRNA. I haven't seen him for a week.

GATES. Go on.

MYRNA. Er. Yes. Tuesday last. He took 'Modern Pedagogy' with me.

This week he didn't show.

GATES. What about the refectory?

MYRNA. Oh, I looked out for him, the same. I think maybe he started to bring in his own food. Apparently he's quit the International Club too. And he's moved out of his room in Wilson Hall.

May I go now, I have class?

GATES. You can skip class.

MYRNA. Sorry?

GATES *lights his pipe.*

GATES. I've been thinking a good deal about trust lately. What does it rest on? A certain confidence in people, in institutions, derived from benign experiences of precisely those things. Maybe these qualities are quintessentially American qualities. I think – without I hope being chauvinist, Myrna – you, like so many of the kids in this country, tend to think the best of others, of our leaders, of our nation, and of folks from other nations. I consider it a great strength. But perhaps at times it may make us seem obtuse – blind to how the other person feels. Also, incapable of intimating their intentions and their suspicions, such as they are.

MYRNA. I, I slightly feel what little trust I had established with Mr Qutb I have... abused. In coming here. And in fact I would like to be excused from my... from this – role.

GATES. Of course. When we finish the debrief.

Did you never find out his purpose in being here?

MYRNA. As I said, he was very evasive.

GATES. Did he ever mention any organisation he was connected with?

MYRNA. No. I don't believe so, no.

GATES. He didn't mention any publications he was involved with?

MYRNA. Oh. He mentioned a journal, way back, I told you.

GATES. Now – this is serious. Did he ever mention a group called the Moslem Brotherhood at all? Or a man called Hassan al-Banna? Do you recall that name, at all.

Pause.

Myrna?

MYRNA. Possibly.

GATES. Possibly?

MYRNA. Why would it matter, he has a right to his beliefs, don't we all, First Amendment!

GATES. The Brotherhood in itself sounds fairly harmless, but in fact these believers don't just meet and praise Allah, oh no, they, and there are many of them, well, for one thing they have a militia of their own, Myrna, now why do you think they might need a militia –

MYRNA. I have no idea and I really don't see what this has to do with us, here.

GATES. Yes apparently they seem intent on returning their country, and who knows even ours in time, to the pristine days of the seventh century, to reinstate laws framed by men in deserts, and yes, even now they stop movie showings, they set alight the residencies of the British, of foreigners, they've even burned a book or two –

MYRNA. Well, I am sure they have their reasons. I hardly think these British are in Egypt for the fun of it. Maybe, maybe Egypt needs its revolution, maybe – I mean, I think we had one once, I guess we wanted to kick out the British too –

GATES. Good answer, good answer. And you know, it may not be a bad thing. Let them have their backward-looking beliefs, maybe it'll keep them from communism, right? But these are the stakes, Myrna. This country can no longer afford its lofty innocence, its clean hands – because we have enemies, more than ever before. So we need friends as never before. All over the world. All over the world, Myrna.

Pause. A bell goes for class.

MYRNA. I just don't like to think of myself as some sort of spy.

GATES. You're not a spy. A spy tells lies. You haven't told any lies. A spy receives payment. A spy works against the interests of those they spy on. You're a friend. We are all his friends. We've extended the hand of friendship to Mr Qutb, thrown the door wide and invited him in and he's come on in, run up to his bedroom and slammed that door in our face.

Pause.

Look, I can see you don't like this, I understand your reasons for that, I respect your reasons.

MYRNA. I take it there's something you want me to find out, some specific thing.

Pause.

GATES. He's moved to private lodgings on the corner of Fifth and Tenth. The landlady has made contact with us. You know her. She taught you. It would be good if you could... drop by.

MYRNA. 'Drop by'?

GATES. Yes. She can let you in to his room.

It would be useful to know what he's reading. What he's thinking about.

MYRNA. What if he won't receive me? What if he comes back and finds me?

GATES. In that instance you might need to assume a role.

MYRNA. I don't understand.

GATES. Oh, sure you do, Myrna. He's a lonely guy. I think he would appreciate company. The company of a woman.

Scene Four

Night, a day later. PHILIP's office. Boxes of packed books, which overlap with the books in SAYYID's room. LAYLA unveiled, dishevelled. She has a number of carrier bags with her. As LAYLA enters, MYRNA also enters a gloomy-looking room, cold, barely used; piles of papers and books everywhere. MYRNA finds a document. Throughout the scene, MYRNA sifts documents. LAYLA is reading something on PHILIP's laptop; PHILIP enters with a bag of food.

PHILIP. How did you get in?

LAYLA. Your door was unlocked.

PHILIP. I mean on campus.

LAYLA. The library remains open through the night.

PHILIP. Did anyone see you?

LAYLA. No one recognises me like this.

She puts her hijab back on.

I hid in the prayer room, then the library.

PHILIP. I tried to reach you – wanted to warn you not to go back to your flat –

LAYLA. You did not email me.

PHILIP. I couldn't, my emails are being tagged.

LAYLA. They searched my room – but you know this?

They robbed me, stole my laptop, my clothes, my Qur'ān even – why, why take that?

PHILIP. I had absolutely no part in any of that –

LAYLA. Hiding like a spy, seated, hours on end, in the dark library. This is your academic freedom!

PHILIP. We shouldn't be doing even this. The Dean's suspending me until I disclose everything to do with you.

LAYLA. What are you afraid of? Do you think I am here to commit a martyrdom operation? Would I not have acted before now? Is my veil so dangerous to you? A piece of cloth, a tool of modesty! Or, no, maybe it is my example – a thinking woman who is not some sort of shrill feminist, an Egyptian woman who does not worship the West, a believer in a world of unbelief.

PHILIP. All of the above; but you can't stay here long.

So you read it?

LAYLA. Yes.

PHILIP. Then you'll have seen it's a fucking mess. References all over the shop, every other word 'perhaps' or 'what if', a jigsaw with all the key pieces missing. You haven't been honest with me, Layla.

LAYLA. I gave you everything that could be read.

PHILIP. No, I don't think so. Here's one mystery for starters: okay, there are references in several letters, let's see, 10th December, just before he leaves Greeley, to Hamina, then 12th when he's en route to California, references back to a letter – yeah – here we go –

He checks the laptop.

LAYLA. You scanned them on to your computer?

PHILIP. Of course. And taken multiple copies.

LAYLA. I did not say you could do this.

PHILIP. Tough, it's what I do. So, the 10th: 'The letter I sent yesterday. Destroy it.' Okay? And then, from her, the 19th: 'The disgrace is not yours, brother.' Where's the letter on the 9th?

LAYLA. She abided by his wishes.

PHILIP. He often asks her to destroy letters and she patently didn't, I'm sorry, I think you're lying about this –

LAYLA. If there is a letter, it would refer merely to academic matters.

PHILIP. 'If', 'if'? Bullshit! Now that's – you know that's bullshit.

LAYLA. Philip, your language is becoming coarse.

PHILIP. Plus someone's been doctoring it – look, here, in November, stuff about 'M'. Lines blanked out. 'M', 'M' – clearly a woman –

LAYLA. I have no idea to whom this refers.

PHILIP. He says a woman comes to him, recruits him, later, he speaks of a woman who refers to sex as a 'biological' matter.

LAYLA. Philip, do you see what you are doing? This is the problem with your book – it is not written in the correct spirit. It is written with a cheap aim: to blacken a great man's reputation –

PHILIP. Maybe you'd prefer the whole myth of him not 'succumbing to the West'?

LAYLA. He did not succumb, he experienced but did not succumb, it is plain to see, he did not succumb.

PHILIP. How would you know? You have evidence for that?

LAYLA. I know, I know.

PHILIP. No, you're lying now. You're lying, and worse, you're kidding yourself. Give me the missing letter.

LAYLA. How infantile this scholarship is! As if one letter could besmirch a man of impeccable purity.

PHILIP. There is one. Isn't there? Isn't there?

LAYLA. I gave you these letters on the understanding you would treat me as a colleague, enable my studies.

PHILIP. If you hadn't started wreaking havoc, spreading rumours, dragging my name in the dirt –

LAYLA. Am I responsible for what others do?

Do you not recognise the pressures upon me?

PHILIP. I have no idea, no idea what the truth is about you any more.

Pause.

LAYLA. I have some notes. Concerning your manuscript. If you implement those notes, trust may be re-established between us.

Pause.

PHILIP. Okay. Right. So now you want me to, what, change my book – to, what, censor it?

LAYLA. Merely to change its emphasis.

PHILIP. Hang on: what is this? Is this you? Is this *you* speaking?

LAYLA. Who else would it be?

PHILIP. Why did you come here, Layla? Why did you ever come here?

LAYLA. To guide you. Here is your guidance.

LAYLA hands him a folded piece of typescript.

In 1949; SAYYID *comes into the space to* MYRNA *– she stands, uncertain. He is amazed.*

MYRNA. Sorry. She – your landlady let me in.

SAYYID. You!

MYRNA. You see, I know Mrs Martinez, she taught me. Of course, Greeley is a small town.

SAYYID. This is male accommodation. Please. You must leave now.

MYRNA. Okay. Sure. Gosh, such a small room. For you. So impersonal. You deserve better. I am sure Professor Gates, if you asked, could get you a bachelor apartment –

SAYYID. It is sufficient, what I need, no more.

MYRNA. Right. But so far off campus?

For what, for privacy?

SAYYID. Of course for privacy, of course. Do you come here to interrogate me?

MYRNA. No. We just miss you up there.

SAYYID. Miss me?

MYRNA. Yes. Been looking out for you. In the refectory. Eating a whole lot of melon too. With, with the pepper.

SAYYID. Melon? Have you been drinking, Miss Bailey?

MYRNA. You know, I thought there might be a picture of someone here. I guess I was being nosy again, I am very – kind of – yeah, I expected to see – a loved one.

SAYYID. Images are idolatrous.

MYRNA. But a woman, maybe. I guess I thought you might have a wife. Given your age. You don't wear a band.

SAYYID. No. I am not. I do not have a – why would this concern you?

MYRNA. Why would it not? I do, I genuinely care.

SAYYID. You have a fiancé.

MYRNA. Not any more, matter of fact. Wayne's kind of possessive. Tribute to you. Oh, he finds you to be the most enormous threat. Not alone in that.

SAYYID. He is a fool to think so, what have I done but… I have not done a thing.

MYRNA. Oh, I agree. I agree with that.

Pause.

SAYYID. Please, it is not right – we could walk –

MYRNA. I do find I can say things, think things with you. Since we met, day to day, everything, everything feels so different. Like Pastor Gates – gosh, I used to admire him so much, but now...? You know, is that belief? God, and he's a hypocrite, with all his apparent tolerance, can it be true tolerance if the first time it's tested... you see this, this is what I'm like. Since I met you.

She touches his hand; he lets her but freezes.

Gosh, I just keep doing that – I know I am very young and very foolish and you, you're a very serious person and I entirely, completely respect that, I value that, but I do like to touch your hand.

He takes it away. Then snatches hers back and kisses it.

LAYLA *and* PHILIP.

PHILIP. Who wrote this? You?

LAYLA. Of course.

PHILIP. No, this is not you. Not your voice.

LAYLA. Who else could it be? Please.

PHILIP. It's him, isn't it? Your brother.

Of course – you sent him my manuscript.

I see, I see, is this what this is about? You are here effectively as his, what, his conduit, you function as a...

LAYLA. Philip, do you agree to the terms stated?

PHILIP. What?

LAYLA. Do you agree to the conditions?

PHILIP. Oh. Do I agree to these very useful notes?

Well, thank you and thank him for me. Okay, let's see, let's get this clear, so you wish, nay require, me to emphasise Qutb's links with the Brotherhood before his time in America even though he didn't join until 1953, which would be a lie, would it not, but why let the truth get in the way of the myth, you want me to show how he presciently witnessed the sham of American life, always stressing his purity, stressing his piety, stressing his ideological correctness all down the line –

LAYLA. He was a believer from the outset. He was sent to America because of his movement towards the Brotherhood. In America his convictions were only confirmed. He, we are not asking you to change the substance of your book – this is your book.

PHILIP. You or him? Are you in complete agreement? Or has he bullied you to do this?

LAYLA. We simply ask you to change the emphasis of it.

We do not question your fitness for the task; we think it is a very important book at a crucial time.

PHILIP. Ah, but you do like to flatter.

LAYLA. We only ask you to rein in your sensationalist interpretations, to submit to the obvious and clear pathway he took, which will result in a far superior book which we would not feel we had to condemn.

PHILIP. Okay. 'Condemn.' Right. And what form would such a condemnation take?

Pause.

We're not talking a dusty review on Amazon? Okay – so would it perhaps take the form of a clerical condemnation? Course, you can't take me out, I'm a kafir, but maybe my readers, my translators, any library that stocks it, intimidate them, that sort of condemnation?

LAYLA. As you speak of intimidation, we also feel it would be appropriate for you to reflect on your own part in the continuing suppression of the Brotherhood, namely your role at the AUC during the years 2001 to 2011.

Pause.

PHILIP. Right – what, what role was that exactly?

LAYLA. You do not need me to elaborate. It is likely in the forthcoming weeks and years that documentation between you, your superiors there and the security forces will come to light. This will not reflect well on you. Were you to make this book a kind of apologia, that damage might be mitigated.

Silence.

PHILIP. Okay. Let's be clear, okay, I was required, we were all required to keep pastoral notes on all our students.

Pause.

I did no more nor less than my colleagues.

As a matter of fact, I defended the right to protest, I engaged with them, that's what I've always done, I have engaged. What my superiors did with those notes… even now.

LAYLA. I would respect your desire for truth more if you were yourself truthful.

Silence.

Of all the violations for myself, the worst was the virginity test. Kicking and screaming all the way to the military facility. The doctor I do not blame but I cannot forgive. May his vile fingers wither for their actions! Of course their filthy minds found nothing to feed on, nothing. And unlike my brother, I was not actually raped. But then for generations they have broken our bones, torn off our veils and ripped out our beards and nails and see, we only grow stronger!

Pause.

I expect now you agree to those terms?

MYRNA *and* SAYYID*;* SAYYID *stands.*

SAYYID. You came to this room to make advances? Of a sexual nature? You entered into my private room?

MYRNA. Sure, isn't it – I didn't plan to, Sayyid –

SAYYID. I would prefer that you use my full name. I would prefer that you acknowledge I am a man, a grown man with a full name.

MYRNA. This is. I have been. I'm so… sorry – I – have I breached something, some – because I had no intention not the slightest…

SAYYID. But you are a practical person from a practical people, I expect you have taken measures –

MYRNA. 'Measures'? Sorry?

SAYYID. Birth-control measures, huh, you perhaps have a wire inside of you –

MYRNA. What? No – a wire? This is crazy!

SAYYID. A coil, mmm, no, or perhaps a rubber receptacle for my seed, in which to deposit my –

MYRNA. Good God, no, no – what do you think I am?

SAYYID. I expect you – now – of course – you had intended all along, all along –

MYRNA. Why are you so angry about this? I honestly can't speak from experience, but isn't… sex… just such a sweet, a lovely thing, and I have to say I have never been – y'know – I have never done anything – yes, Wayne kissed me, petted with me once or twice –

SAYYID. Yes, yes, this young man, you make yourself his chattel –

MYRNA. No, nothing… put his hand where he oughtn't, and apologised and I only stopped him because I was shy, but I just don't feel that way with you because you seem – I didn't come here to do – to seduce you. I wouldn't know how – but if I felt for you, if I felt something for you – Sayyid!

She touches him again; SAYYID *releases a terrible cry.*

SAYYID. Call me by my full name!

She stands.

MYRNA. I'm sorry. I'm sorry. Okay. Maybe you don't like… girls. That's fine, that's okay. I see, I made a mistake, I surely – but it's okay about that if –

SAYYID. Now get out, get out.

MYRNA. Okay, I will I will but I have to tell you, okay – I did not come here for that reason. No, no, in point of fact I was asked to come here!

Pause.

SAYYID. You were… asked? To do this?

MYRNA. Not this. But this, to – yes. Yes I was, yes.

SAYYID. To come to my room?

You were asked to spy on me?

MYRNA. Yes – no – well, yes I have, yes. But not just, not just
me, not, not only me, I am sorry – are we, do you consider us
your enemies now? I didn't want – I did it because I wanted
to look out for you, and sure I recognise I have been used but
that wasn't why – that wasn't what I – intended.

SAYYID *is dumbstruck; then he begins to pack, hastily.*

What are you doing? Mr Qutb? You're not – leaving? Why
are you packing? You don't need to do that.

He looks at her.

SAYYID. This is the House of War.

MYRNA. I didn't catch that.

SAYYID. Everything I have done before will be undone.

MYRNA. Please, there's no need to be precipitate, really.

SAYYID. What have I been doing all these years? Books,
literature, writing, these words, for whom were they written,
these acts of vanity?

MYRNA. Sayyid, you're talking – in Arabic, I couldn't – I
think we all here, in the end we would like to help you.

He looks at her as if he had forgotten her presence.

SAYYID. I thank you, Miss Myrna Bailey, and I thank your
professors and your intended and your progressive pedagogy
for teaching me the lesson I have sought to evade all these
years, that I am corrupted from top to toe by your corruption,
that you have made me want what you want and filled my
mind with your hollow dreams and from this day, in your
actions, how clear it all seems to me, how the sweet bite
turns foul in the mouth, look at you, you are aglow, your
body is in flames, look at you signalling to me through fire,
not even aware that your skin is ablaze, thank you for
teaching me the lesson I have always known but been too
weak to admit – from now on I submit to an authority that
makes all your maxims and actions ludicrous.

MYRNA. You're not, you're not making any sense to me at all, at all. I feel there's been a terrible misunderstanding. Mr Qutb, please.

SAYYID *exits*.

Perhaps we can just start over again. Because there are mistakes on all sides here. Mr Qutb! Mr Qutb!

A choir sings:

CHOIR.
    Ah, well, I remember
    Friends of purple and gold
    Friends met in September
    Pledging their faith to hold
    Come friends of September
    Come dear friends of old
    Time shall never sever
    Friends of purple and gold.

The stage is empty except for PHILIP *and* LAYLA.

PHILIP. Yes, I wrote to my Head of Department about him. Your brother. Noting his brilliance. Noting his charisma. Noting his influence on his peers.

And, okay, that he might need to be… watched. That he might be dangerous. He'd written this wild essay about… Qutb. I even copied it. All about his purity. 'The rubbish heap of the West.' Yeah. All about how he had been misunderstood, betrayed. I cited… the essay. Exhibit A.

Pause.

And I stand by that assessment but, no, not… not what probably, what inevitably followed.

Sorry. The default liberal position.

Pause.

I can't write this book.

I'd have to start all over again. All over again. I'd have to be somebody else altogether.

LAYLA. What are you saying?

PHILIP. It's very simple. I don't understand him. Simple as that. Him or you, in fact. How do you write a book about a man who's a closed book?

Laughs.

I'd have to understand faith. Grievance. Hurt. Have to fear women, sex, freedom, I don't fear it, I relish it. What have I been doing, writing the guy in my own image, not seeing him for my shadow?

No, can't be done, not by me.

Pause.

Maybe you can do it, though.

LAYLA. Now you are taunting me again.

PHILIP. You're not standing in your own light. But were you to do it, you'd have to have the guts to tell the truth.

LAYLA. I am not a scholar, you said so yourself.

PHILIP. Isn't this the time to test their appetite for truth? You know you've acquired it, bitten that apple. And you know that taste, it's got nothing to do with the West. Nothing whatsoever.

Pause.

LAYLA. There was another letter.

Pause.

I had to – destroy it. This letter.

I read it. Then I burned it.

Pause.

PHILIP. Oh, Layla.

Pause.

LAYLA. A woman came to him. He was tempted and he faltered. Why must we know that he faltered?

PHILIP. Ah. Why indeed?

LAYLA. The story would only be sad, then.

PHILIP. Why is that?

LAYLA. That a man of his gifts would die untouched.

That a great idea might come from weakness.

PHILIP. That he was a human being.

Pause.

Sound off of traffic. Light at the window.

Okay. Maybe you'd better – I think it would be better if
you –

LAYLA. Of course. I am compromising you.

PHILIP. Oh no. No, don't worry about that. I doubt I'll survive
this one. I can – I'll call you a cab. It's so early. Smuggle you
out.

LAYLA. There is no need.

PHILIP. And actually I mean have you even enough – money –
for a flight? I can –

LAYLA. Oh, it is a condition of study for me, Philip. The return
flight. I keep it with me at all times.

PHILIP. Of course. 'A condition of study.'

LAYLA *gathers her things, and then the letters.*

In the end, this, it's about what you fought for, Layla, isn't
it? Was it for the right to elect a free government or the right
to elect a bunch of people deputising for God? Was it really
for freedom from oppression or just a change in oppressors?
That's what it's about, all this.

LAYLA. You have no right to ask such questions.

PHILIP. I know. I'm aware of that at least.

LAYLA. You know, I pity you, Philip. God has no part in your
life. And you have found nothing to replace him with. All
you have is a morality that lasts no longer than an impulse.
Can a society rest upon such frail foundations?

But – you opened your door to me. I may not contemplate what would have occurred if you had not done so.

To that extent, I wish you well.

He nods. She leaves. He looks after her.

PHILIP. Well. Layla. I wish you well too.

In Egypt.

Blackout.

End.

www.nickhernbooks.co.uk

facebook.com/nickhernbooks

twitter.com/nickhernbooks